MW00377427

BARCELONA

A PHOTOGRAPHIC TOUR

From the PHOTOGRAPHIC TOURS series

ALEXANDRU CIOBANU

2015

Copyright © 2015 by Alexandru Ciobanu
All rights reserved.

This book or any portion thereof may not be reproduced or used in any manner whatsoever without the express written permission of the author or the publisher except for the use of brief quotations in a book review. Although every precaution has been taken to verify the accuracy of the information contained herein, the author and publisher assume no responsibility for any errors or omissions. No liability is assumed for damages that may result from the use of information contained within.

Printed by Amazon. First Printing, 2015
ISBN-13: 978-1517621162
ISBN-10: 151762116X

A collection by Alexandru Ciobanu
Lausanne, Switzerland

From the series Photographic tours

Also available in eBook format

Contact: alexandru.ciobanu.books@gmail.com

www.alexandru-ciobanu.com *www.alexandruciobanubooks.wordpress.com*

TABLE OF CONTENTS

5 BARCELONA THE CITY OF COLORS

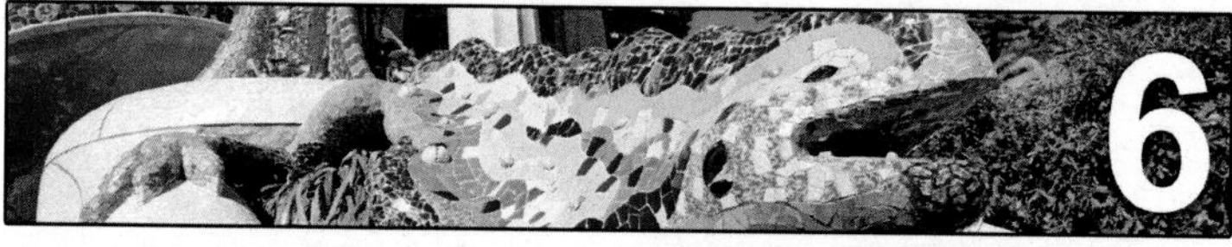

6 GAUDI'S BARCELONA

21 LAS RAMBLAS

25 PORT VELL

35 SQUARES

48 THE OLD TOWN

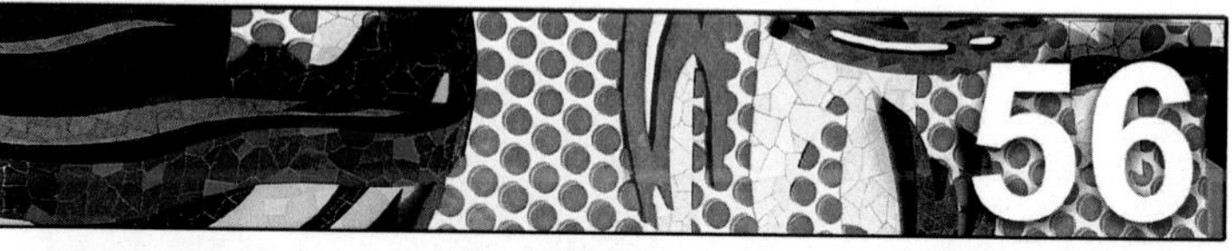

56 ARTISTS AND MUSEUMS

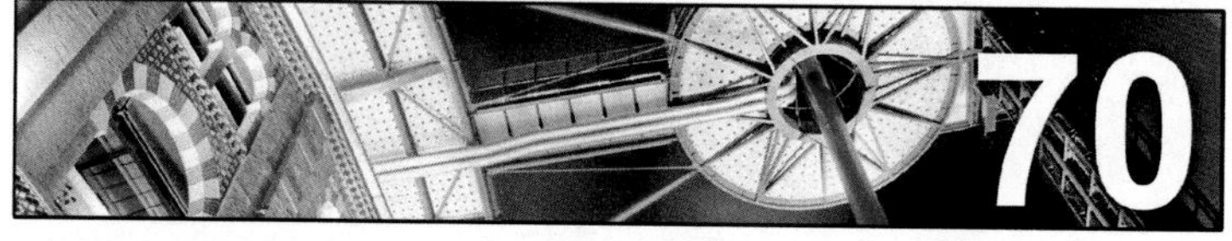

70 THE MODERN CITY

80 THE MONJUIC HILL

86 OUTSIDE THE CITY CENTER

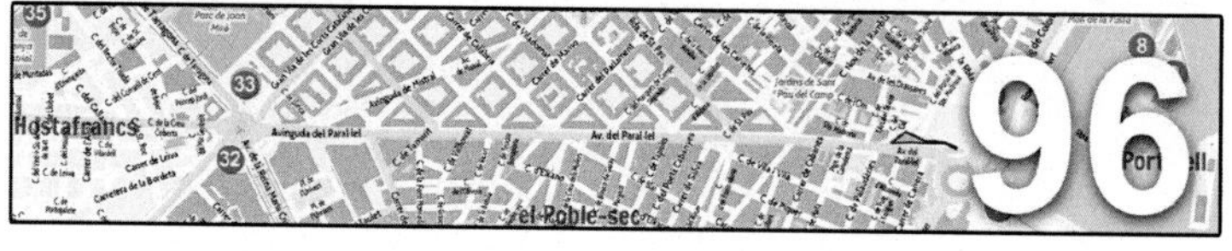

96 MAPS

BARCELONA - THE CITY OF COLORS

Barcelona is the city of colors. The vibrant blue of the Mediterranean Sea and the green of the relaxing parks combine pleasantly with the multicolored facades of the Modernist buildings. This place is bursting with life, energy and joy. Barcelona has a young spirit and it offers a unique mix of attractions, from amazing architecture to medieval cathedrals and world-recognized modern art. With a history that stretches back more than 2000 years, Barcelona keeps reinventing itself over and over again, evolving into an original cosmopolitan mix that makes it one of the most desirable cities on the planet.

Here art is everywhere, as the city is home to a number of amazing artists. This is the place where the heritage of the famous architect, Antoni Gaudi, can be admired in all its greatness. Sagrada Familia, Casa Batllo and Parc Guell are only some of his creations. Juan Miró is another famous Catalan artist, native to Barcelona, whose works have strongly influenced the city.

The heart of the city is the Las Ramblas Boulevard. Located centrally and very popular, this street offers a wide range of attractions, cultural venues, restaurants, the famous "human statues" and the colorful Boqueria market. Close to here, the visitor may admire the historical buildings of the old town. Dating back to medieval times, small intricate streets guide the traveler to monumental landmarks, such as the Barcelona Cathedral and the Santa Maria del Mar church, both marvelous examples of Catalan Gothic architecture. After a stroll through the old town, you can admire the modern part of the city and indulge in the many amazing architectural works located throughout Barcelona.

But the city of Barcelona has even more to offer. There are numerous attractive beaches, where locals and tourists alike relax on hot summer days. The city has a large number of museums covering a wide range of subjects, from history and science to famous artists such as Pablo Picasso and Juan Miró. Barcelona has also a lot to offer for nature lovers. You can go walking up the Montjuic hill and admire the city from a bird's eye view, you can relax in the many parks around the city and you can even visit places outside Barcelona, such as the Tibidabo mountain and the Monserrat monastery.

This book will guide your steps through a visual journey of the city of Barcelona, and you will have the chance to admire amazing photographs of all the important places, monuments and landmarks. It is a wonderful opportunity to indulge in the heart of Barcelona and feel the Catalan culture and Mediterranean atmosphere of this inviting city.

Gaudi's Barcelona

Barcelona is without doubt associated with Antoni Gaudi, the famous architect that lived between 1852 and 1926. Most of his works are located in Barcelona, and he changed the face of the city forever. His style was shaped by neo-Gothic and oriental influences but also by his love of nature.

The most important and famous work of Gaudi is most certainly the Sagrada Familia church (1). Construction of this impressive structure commenced in 1882, but it was not finished and is still in construction today.

The architectural style of the building is Catalan Modernism. Gaudi designed an elegant system of interior columns (2) and richly decorated the church with original sculptures, which represent both religious figures and scenes (3 and 4). Another characteristic of Sagrada Familia is the abundance of towers, eight completed so far from the total of eighteen initially planned by Gaudi. The towers are decorated with colorful geometric shapes, reminding us of the Cubist architecture (5).

The imposing Sagrada Familia can easily be seen from many parts of the city (6), especially from the high viewing points, like the Montjuic hill.

Antoni Gaudi also designed the amazing Park Güell, one of the most important attractions of the city. It is a public garden which offers beautiful landscapes and amazing architectonic elements.

At the center of the monumental ensemble from the park is the beautiful and richly-decorated dragon stairway (7). This stairway leads the visitors toward the Greek theater or the Plaza (8), a big square situated at a high level, which offers beautiful views over the park and the city. The Plaza is bordered by a long serpentine bench richly-decorated with colorful mosaics.

The beauty of the park is completed by the two pavilions that look like amazing fairytale houses (9). Located at the southern entrance, they have colorful roofs of mosaic-patterned Catalan tiles. The mosaics represent a central theme of the park and they can be seen everywhere (10 - 12).

Park Güell is richly-decorated with large stone columns, with an organic appearance which often take on human shape (13).

One iconic feature of the park is the dragon fountain (14). The smiling dragon is decorated with colored ceramic tiles and is a symbol of fire and alchemy.

1

2

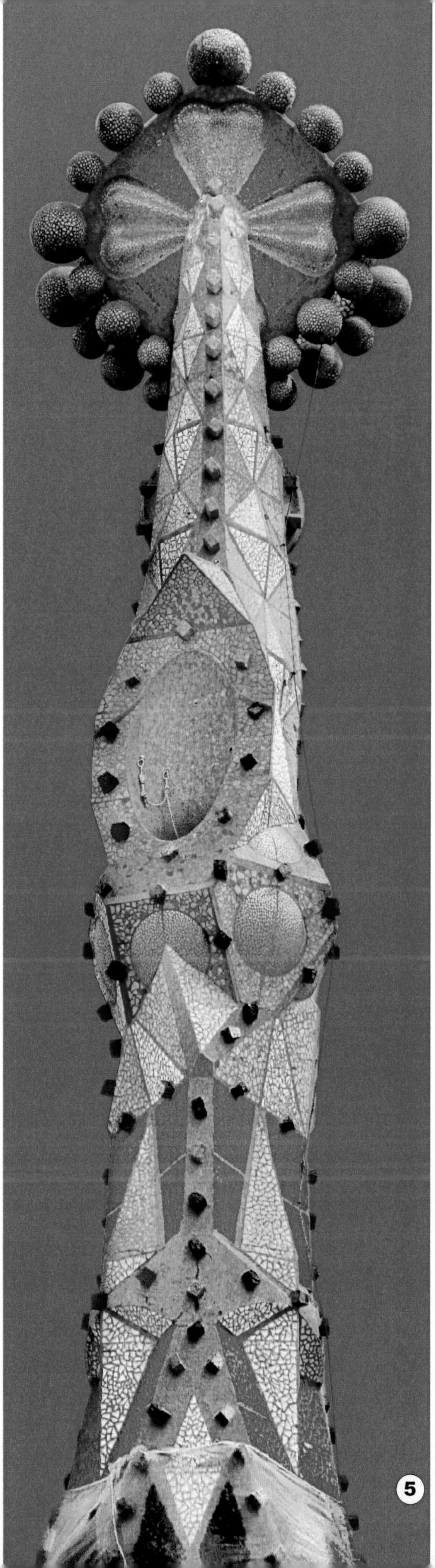

5

6

7

Apart from the unique architectural elements found here, Park Güell is also a complex garden, offering beautiful Mediterranean landscapes (15) and places for relaxation, all elegantly interconnected with the architecture.

Antoni Gaudi left his mark in different places in Barcelona. He designed several iconic houses, such as Casa Batlló, Casa Milà, Casa Vicens, Palau Güell and the Güell Pavilions, to name just a few. The most renowned are the first two.

Casa Batlló is one of Gaudi's masterpieces. The facade of this Modernist building is beautifully decorated with colorful ceramic pieces (16), the roof has an arched profile and the shape, together with the ceramic tiles, make it look like the back of a dragon (17). The chimney stacks on the rooftop have intriguing shapes and colors (18).

In agreement with the facade, for the interior, Gaudi used his imagination, originality and genius to decorate the rooms using beautiful, elaborately-shaped elements (19-22).

Casa Milà, also known as La Pedrera, is another famous work of Antoni Gaudi. As it is the case for many other buildings signed by the architect, it is a UNESCO Cultural World Heritage site. It has an undulating stone facade (23) and the balconies and windows contain metallic decorations made of twisting wrought iron.

The rooftop is fabulous, with strangely-shaped chimneys and vents which give the house a fantastic, dreamy look (24).

9

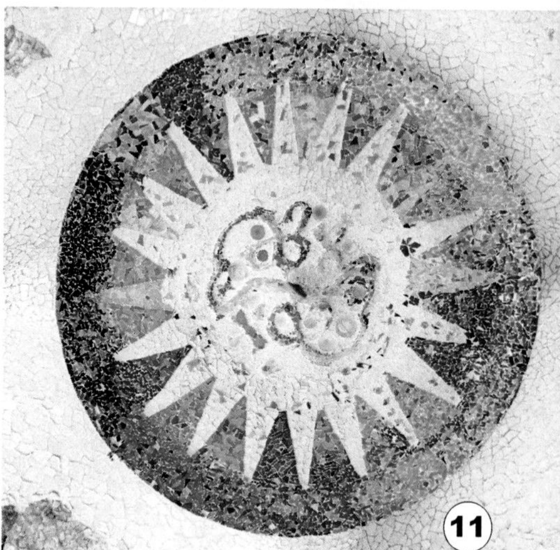

14

15

18

19

20

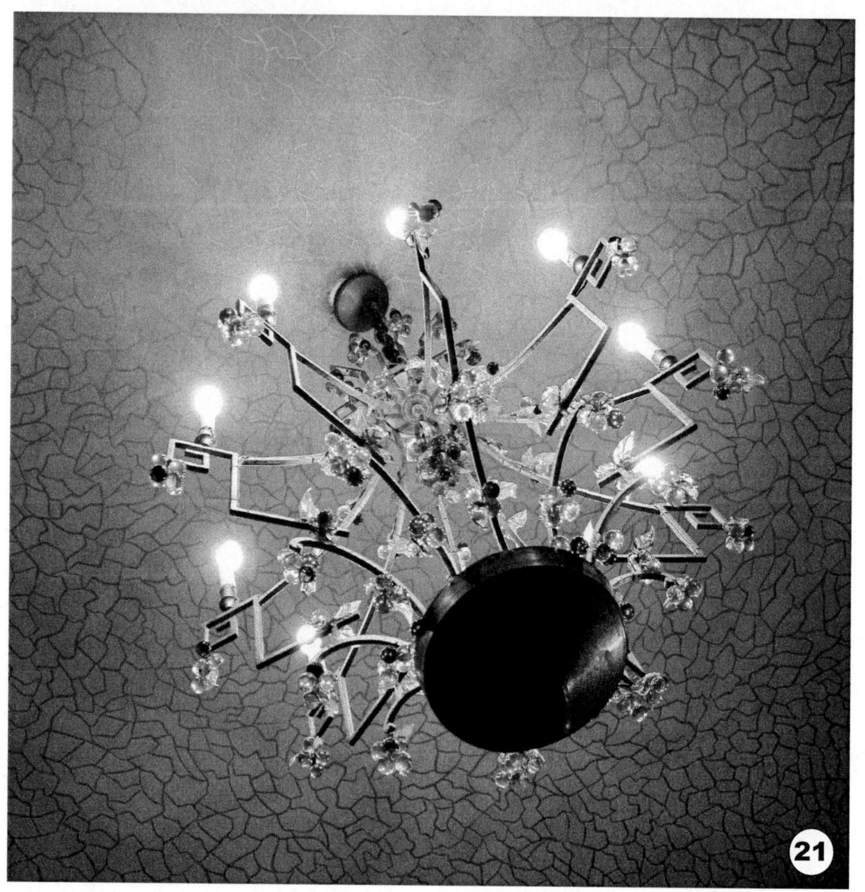

21

22

23

24

Las Ramblas

The main street in the center of Barcelona is Las Ramblas, a large avenue which swirls like a giant green snake between the buildings (25). This is actually a 1.2 km (0.75 miles) long complex of smaller streets.

Picturesque buildings line this street (26) about which the Spanish poet Federico García Lorca said is “the only street in the world which I wish would never end”.

At the lower end of the boulevard, close to the seaside, is the monument of Columbus (27 - 29). Erected in 1888, it is 60 meters (197 feet) tall and it celebrates the first voyage of the explorer Christopher Columbus who, after his trip, returned to Barcelona to report his discoveries.

Walking down Las Ramblas, one can see the emblematic street performers posing as “human statues” (30 - 31).

These artists are really imaginative, they have original costumes which are often very elaborated, and they have to stay still, moving only when someone offers them a coin in sign of appreciation.

change
PARIS
Santander
Santander
Santander

26

27

28

29

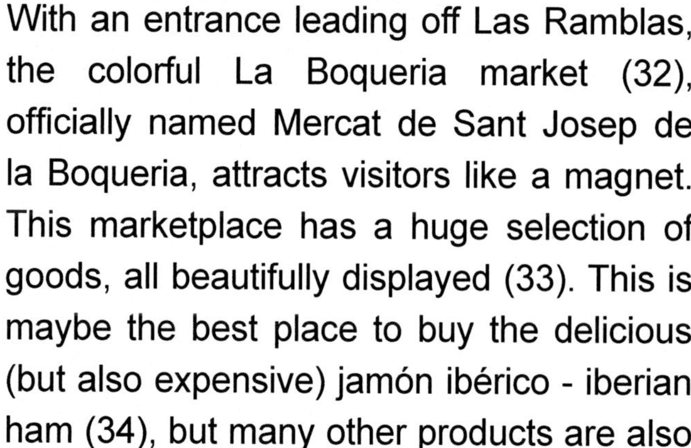

With an entrance leading off Las Ramblas, the colorful La Boqueria market (32), officially named Mercat de Sant Josep de la Boqueria, attracts visitors like a magnet. This marketplace has a huge selection of goods, all beautifully displayed (33). This is maybe the best place to buy the delicious (but also expensive) jamón ibérico - iberian ham (34), but many other products are also sold here, such as fresh vegetables, fruits and sweets (35).

The market has a long history, the first mention of it dating back as far as 1217. Probably the most interesting part of the market is the fish section, where fresh seafood, fish and lobsters are available daily (36-38).

Port Vell

Las Ramblas Boulevard ends at the Mediterranean Sea, at Port Vell, the touristy part of the Port of Barcelona. At the entrance to the port area, there is the Old Customs building (39), an elegant construction in the Neoclassical style, finished in 1902.

Until 1992, this area was an obsolete harbor, with empty warehouses and not so pretty industrial buildings. After its renewal for the 1992 Barcelona Olympics, it is now a major landmark of the city, featuring a beautiful wooden pedestrian bridge, Rambla de Mar (40), a fancy port for small boats (Port Olympic, 41), several old historical buildings and a beautiful promenade which heads toward the Barceloneta neighborhood.

32

33

34

36

35

37

38

PORT DE BARCELONA

39

Close by is the Jaume I tower (42), the second stop of the Port Vell aerial tramway, officially named Transbordador Aeri del Port, a cable car transporting people from the port area to the Montjuic hill. At 107 meters (351 feet), the tower is the second tallest aerial lift pylon in the world, which points to the fact that riding this aerial cable car is not for the faint-hearted!

The most popular attraction at Port Vell is certainly the aquarium (43), considered one of the biggest in Europe. There are 35 aquariums here, beautifully arranged to reproduce different specific ecosystems (44), hosting over 11.000 animals from hundreds of species, including crustaceans, seahorses and piranha (45-48). Yet, Barcelona still has more to offer to nature lovers. In the Parc de la Ciutadella, there is a large zoo (49), home to more than 320 species of animals and, on the Montjuic hill, there is a botanical garden (50) which covers more than 14 hectares.

The waves of the Mediterranean Sea wash across the sandy beaches of Barcelona city (51). In total, there are about 4 km of beaches, close to the city center and organized in four sectors: Barceloneta, Icària, Mar Bella (unofficially a nudist beach) and Sitges (30 minutes outside the city).

40

42

41

Barceloneta beach (52, 53) is the most popular, maybe also due to its location close to the city center, only a few minutes walk from the metro stop with the same name. There are plenty of activities to do here, other than swimming and sunbathing. You can try water sports, such as windsurfing or kite surfing, or enjoy a cold drink at one of the many beach huts. Alternatively, you can take a walk, admiring the local artists creating amazing sand sculptures (54), the interesting artistic monument called "Homenatge a la Barceloneta" (55), or simply experience a romantic sunrise (56).

43

44

45
46
47
48

49

50

SQUARES

Around Barcelona, there are several big squares, very popular and attractive. One of the biggest is Espanya Square (Plaça d'Espanya, 57), which was built for the 1929 International Exposition. It is located at the intersection of several major boulevards, at the base of the Montjuic hill, and the street marked by the two Venetian towers leads the way to the National Palace. The fountain in the middle of the square was designed by Josep Maria Jujol, one of Antoni Gaudi's fellow architects.

The official city center is considered to be the Catalonia Square or Plaça de Catalunya (58). This large square is the starting point of the famous Las Ramblas street and it is beautifully decorated with fountains, sculptures and flowers (59).

Another well-known place, especially for the nightlife, is Reial Square (60), which was designed in the 19th century. Here, there are many restaurants and some of the city's most popular nightclubs. With its palm trees and lamps designed by Gaudi, it is a good place for relaxation, or to simply enjoy a coffee. Also, every Sunday morning, there is a coin and stamp market in this square.

At the junction of the streets Gran Via and Carrer Marina, there is the Plaza del Toros Monumental de Barcelona or, simply, La Monumental (61), a bullring arena inaugurated in 1914. The last bullfight in this bullring was held in 2012 and it was the last place in Catalonia to host such an event, before bullfights were officially banned. It has a capacity of 19,582 places, arranged circularly in 26 rows (62).

51

52

54

BOX220 SURF SHOP

58

59

60

61

THE OLD TOWN

The historic part of Barcelona city is the old town, the Bari Gòtic district (63). Also known as the Gothic district, this is a medieval area located between the boulevards Rambla and Via Leietana. It is characterized by narrow streets, paved with cobbles and lined by tall buildings (64 - 66).

One iconic building is the Neogothic Bridge of Sighs (65), found on Carrer Bisbe. There were many similar bridges here but they were all destroyed in the twentieth century. The one mentioned above is not the original bridge, but a recent reproduction.

Placa del Rei (67) is a famous square located in the heart of the old town. It consists of a large space delimited by an ensemble of gothic buildings, a remainder of the medieval past of the city. This square is surrounded by the architectural complex that forms the Grand Royal Palace (Palau Reial Major), home to kings and counts of Barcelona during the Middle Age. The part of the palace depicted in the photo includes the King Martin's Watchtower (Torre Mirador del Rei Martí) and the gothic structure of Palau del Lloctinent, the home of the lieutenant of the Catalan Parliament. Placa del Rei is a relaxing place and it works like a gateway towards the past, allowing the traveler to experience how life was here during the medieval times.

Almost in the center of the Gothic district stands the Barcelona Cathedral, officially called the Cathedral of the Holy Cross and Saint Eulalia (68 - 70). The construction of this impressive building started in 1298 and it took 150 years to complete. Changes have been made to the Cathedral more recently, such as the Neo-Gothic facade, which was completed in 1890.

The historical heritage of Barcelona is not only found in the Bari Gothic, but also elsewhere in the city. Thus, in the Ribera district, rising between old, narrow streets, is the Santa Maria del Mar, an imposing church dating from 1383 (71). With its monumental columns (72) and the sober facade made in stone, this church is a superb example of Catalan Gothic architecture.

Between medieval cathedrals and famous landmarks, the traveler is spoiled with delicious Mediterranean food, which can be enjoyed in famous places such as the restaurant Els Quatre Gats (The four cats, 73), where personalities such as Pablo Picasso used to spend time, or the renowned Escriba bakery (74). Sea food and fish (75, 76) as well as paella (77), or the popular appetizers called tapas (78), are only a few of the multiple culinary possibilities that Barcelona has to offer.

64

65

66

69

70

72

ARTISTS AND MUSEUMS

Barcelona is the place to be for art lovers. Around the city, there are several unique artworks signed by famous artists. El Cap de Barcelona (79), signed by Roy Lichtenstein, is a surrealist sculpture standing tall in the city center, close to the port. Juan Miró's work, named Woman and Bird (Dona i Ocell, 80) is a 22 meters tall sculpture located in the Joan Miró parc, near Espanya Square. This artist strongly influenced the city and his works welcome the visitors in different parts of Barcelona. One of the most well-known is the circular mosaic from Pla de l'Os, in the center of Rambla (81). Joan Miró initiated the Joan Miró Foundation (82), a museum of contemporary art trying to encourage young artists to experiment.

There are plenty of museums in Barcelona. One of the most visited is the Picasso Museum (83), which houses one of the most extensive collections of artworks signed by the famous Spanish artist.

74

75

76

77

78

Another interesting museum is the Caixa Forum (84), an art gallery located inside a former factory in the Montjuic area. It exhibits various artworks and it is free to visit.

Barcelona is a maritime city, so naturally there is also a Maritime Museum here (85). It is found inside the Gothic building of the Barcelona Royal Shipyard and it offers visitors reproductions of famous ships and artifacts covering naval history from the 1400s to modern times.

Tourists can also visit the Gaudi House Museum (86) which was the residence of the famous architect for almost 20 years, and the Blau Museum of Natural History and Science (Forum Building - 87, 88), which is great for children and has an amazing contemporary look. The list of museums is completed by the National Art Museum of Catalonia (89), one of the most beautiful and most visited museums in the city. Dating from 1929, it is housed in the National Palace (Palau Nacional), a beautiful building with Italian influences.

79

80

81

82

83

84

86

87

88

6

7

CIRCA
CIRCA
CIRCA
BUS
TAXI

THE MODERN CITY

Barcelona is a modern city, living in the present and embracing contemporary trends. Probably the most modern area of Barcelona is the Eixample district, which was constructed at the beginning of the 20th century. It is characterized by buildings with contemporary architecture (90) aligned on long straight streets and displayed in a strict grid pattern (91). The district was designed by the visionary Ildefons Cerdà, who planned the octagonal blocks and the streets in a manner that would provide for optimal traffic, as well as give access to ventilation and sunshine.

The hallmark of Barcelona is the abundance of modernist buildings, as the modernist cultural movement from the beginning of the 20th century was centered here. A fine example of architectural modernism is the Catalan Music Hall building (92), which was, in 1997, declared a UNESCO World Heritage Site. The concert hall is the only one in Europe illuminated by natural light (during daylight hours), through glass panes on the sides and a huge stained-glass skylight (93).

Also a UNESCO World Heritage Site, the Hospital of the Holy Cross and Saint Paul (94, 95) is a typical Modernist ensemble, unique and charming in its beauty. Until 2009, it was a hospital but it is now being transformed into a museum and cultural center. Modernist buildings can take many shapes and sizes. Thus, Casa de les Punxes (House of the Spikes) looks like a Gothic castle (96). It was built between 1903 and 1905 and it is highly appreciated by Modernist lovers.

92

93

94

95

96

97

98

BARCELONA
99

101

102

The streets on the "new" Barcelona are sometimes surprising to the traveler, with original decorations such as the colored tile butterfly from the Modernist Casa Fajol also known as Casa de la Papallona (Butterfly House, 97) and the contemporary street-art located in the most surprising places, like the rooftops of apartment blocks (98).

More recently, the face of the city has been enriched with modern, contemporary buildings. The best known is probably the Torre Agbar (99) a 38-story skyscraper located in the Poblenou neighborhood, representative of the high-tech architecture.

Barcelona is a city with a twist, thus it is no surprise to find here old buildings which are successfully transformed into modern attractions. This is the case of the former bullring arena from Espanya Square, which was converted into the popular Las Arenas shopping center in 2011 (100, 101).

Other modern architectural landmarks of Barcelona are the giant sculpture Fish (Peix, 102), a modern piece of art found in the Olympic port at the base of a skyscraper, and the renowned Camp Nou stadium (103), home of the beloved soccer team, FC Barcelona. With its capacity of 99,354 places, it is the largest stadium in Europe.

100

104

106

107

108

Telefónica

The Montjuic hill

An important landmark in Barcelona is the Monjuic hill (also called the Monjuic mountain), with a height of 184 meters. It is connected to the seaside by an aerial cable car (104), bringing passengers from Port Vell to the top of the hill. Montjuic offers stunning views of the city (105) and typical Mediterranean landscapes (106), so a walking tour in this area is something you will not regret. On the top of the hill is located the Monjuic Castle (107), an ancient military fort with a history that stretches back to 1640. The castle witnessed many battles, was transformed several times and, repeatedly, it was used as a prison and torture chamber.

But Monjuic has more to offer. One of the main attractions here is the Magical Fountain (108), situated next to the National Palace (Palau Nacional). The fountain offers impressive light and music shows in the evenings. Sometimes the show is difficult to see, due to the large crowds of tourists gathering here in full season, but the effort is worthwhile.

Not far away is the Olympic Park, a complex of facilities for sport built for the 1992 Olympic Games in Barcelona. Here, there is an Olympic stadium, an impressive indoor sporting area called Palau Sant Jordi, and also the iconic Telecommunications tower (109), with its interesting shape representing an athlete holding the Olympic torch.

110

111

112

113

114

Finally, at the bottom of the Montjuic Mountain, the traveler reaches the Spanish village (Poble Espanyol), a huge open-air architectural museum, showcasing replicas of houses characteristic for all regions in Spain (110, 111). The space inside the buildings is used in various ways: as ateliers for artisans creating traditional Spanish objects (112), as shops or as restaurants.

Montjuic mountain is basically a huge park filled with attractions and interesting sights. Around the city, there are several smaller parks and gardens, all offering peace and relaxation to visitors. One of the most beautiful is Parc de la Ciutadella (113) which includes a lake, a fountain, museums, the Parliament of Catalonia and the zoo. Interestingly, after its opening in the mid 19th century, it was the only green space of the city. Very close to this park, on Passeig de Lluís Companys, one can admire the Arch of Triumph (114), an astonishing monument built in 1888, in the Neo-Mudéjar style.

115

116

117

118

Another beautiful place is Parc de Cervantes, popular for the beautiful roses growing there (115). There are actually 245 varieties of flowers in this amazing public garden and the roses bloom from April to November, due to the mild climate.

The parks in Barcelona are popular amongst both tourist and locals, who often gather in more quiet places for a game of pétanque (116), a traditional sport that originated in France at the beginning of the 20th century.

These places offer a good alternative to the liveliness of the city. Some parks are home to architectural treasures, such as the Pedralbes Royal Palace (117) from Parc de Pedrables, while others offer nonconformist, controversial landscapes, such as the Parc de L'Espanya Industrial (118).

OUTSIDE THE CITY CENTER

In Barcelona, important attractions are located outside the central area, so it is not a bad idea to venture out of the center in order to visit interesting and sometimes secret places. The Pedralbes monastery (119), a Gothic structure built in 1326, is an amazing attraction situated slightly off the tourist path. The monastery has an impressive 40 meter long cloister (120), formed by wide arches which are sustained by columns.

There are many places around Barcelona which are easy to reach from the city and offer an excellent choice for a day trip. One of them is Montserrat, the Catalan sacred mountain, where the Montserrat monastery is located (121). The mountain is reachable by cable-car (122) and the effort to climb up there is worth it. Besides from the monastery, you will also find here an art museum and a restaurant.

119

120

121

122

Close to the city is the 512 meters (1.680 feet) tall Tibidabo mountain, with its Temple Expiatori del Sagrat Cor church (123) overlooking the city from the summit. The exterior of the church combines a Romanesque fortress of stone (the crypt) with a monumental neo-Gothic church. The interior (124) is incredibly beautiful, with tall decorated columns and artistic stained windows.

Apart from the church, people are also attracted here by the amazing amusement park (125, 126), which both children and adults enjoy alike. The park in itself is not very big, but it offers plenty of fun activities and the views of the city from this point are breathtaking (127).

Colorful, joyful and sunny, Barcelona is attracting people from all over the world. This city has something to offer for everyone, satisfying both the sophisticated traveler and people who are only looking for a fun night out. Whether you are here for a city break, or for a long holiday, enjoy it! Let the Mediterranean sun warm your heart, have fun in the old town, and enjoy the good food and the unique sights Barcelona has to offer. You will not regret it!

CONTRIBUTING PHOTOGRAPHERS

Sagrada Familia facade © Alexandru Ciobanu, photo 1, page 7;

Sagrada Familia © Huci, Fotolia, photo 2, page 8;

Scultures and tower from Sagrada Familia © Alexandru Ciobanu, photos 3 – 5, page 9;

Sagrada Familia from Monjuic © Alexandru Ciobanu, photo 6, page 10;

Stairway at Parc Guell © Alexandru Ciobanu, photo 7, page 10;

The Greek theater from Parc Guell © Alexandru Ciobanu, photo 8, page 11;

Park Guell in Barcelona © Boule1301, Fotolia, photo 9, page 12;

Mosaics at Parc Guell © Alexandru Ciobanu, photos 10 - 12, page 13;

Stonework in Barcelona © Alexandru Ciobanu, photo 13, page 14;

Dragon salamandra of Gaudi in Park Guell © Lunamarina, Canstockphoto, photo 14, page 15;

Landscape in Parc Guell, Barcelona © Alexandru Ciobanu, photo 15, page 15;

Facade of Casa Batllo © Alexandru Ciobanu, photo 16, page 16;

Casa Batllo, roof © Alexandru Ciobanu, photo 17, page 17;

Chimneys at Casa Batllo © Alexandru Ciobanu, photo 18, page 18;

Interior of the famous Casa Batllo building © Bargotiphotography, Canstockphoto, photo 19, page 18;

Decorations inside Casa Batllo © Alexandru Ciobanu, photos 20 - 22, page 19;

Casa Mila in Barcelona © Iakov Filimonov, Dreamstime, photo 23, page 20;

Rooftop of Casa Mila © Alexandru Ciobanu, photo 24, page 20;

Las Ramblas, aerial view © Alexandru Ciobanu, photo 25, page 21;

Picturesque houses at La Rambla © Iakov Filimonov, Dreamstime, photo 26, pages 22 – 23;

Monument of Columbus © Alexandru Ciobanu, photo 27, page 24;

Columbus monument in Barcelona, Spain © Al La, Canstockphoto, photo 28, page 24;

Monument to Christopher Columbus - Barcelona © Alberto Masnovo, Dreamstime, photo 29, page 24;

Human statue © Alexandru Ciobanu, photo 30, page 25;

Human statue on Las Ramblas © Alexandru Ciobanu, photo 31, page 25;

La Boqueria, Barcelona, Spain © Oscar Espinosa Villegas, Dreamstime, photo 32, page 26;

La Boqueria market, Barcelona, Spain © Luciano Mortula, Dreamstime, photo 33, page 26;

La Boqueria market in Barcelona © Byelikova, Dreamstime, photo 34, page 27;

La Boqueria sweets © Roman Borodaev, Dreamstime, photo 35, page 27

Fish market at Boqueria © Alexandru Ciobanu, photo 36, page 27;

Lobster on ice © Alexandru Ciobanu, photo 37, page 27;

Fish at La Boqueria market © Alexandru Ciobanu, photo 38, page 27;

Building at Port Vell © Alexandru Ciobanu, photo 39, pages 28 - 29;

Rambla del Mar © Alexandru Ciobanu, photo 40, page 30;

Port Olympic © Alexandru Ciobanu, photo 41 pages 30-31;

The top view on seaport © Konstik, Canstockphoto, photo 42, page 31;

Barcelona Aquarium © Alexandru Ciobanu, photo 43, page 32;

Seascape at Barcelona Aquarium © Alexandru Ciobanu, photo 44, page 32;

Marine life from Barcelona aquarium © Alexandru Ciobanu, photos 45 - 48, page 33;

Feeding penguins in Zoo De Barcelona © Nejron, Canstockphoto, photo 49, page 34;

View of Botanical garden of Barcelona © Iakov Filimonov, Dreamstime, photo 50, page 34;

Barceloneta beach © Alexandru Ciobanu, photo 51, page 35;

Walking by the sea © Alexandru Ciobanu, photo 52, pages 36-37;

Barceloneta beach and neighborhood © Alexandru Ciobanu, photo 53, page 36;

Sand sculpture © Alexandru Ciobanu, photo 54, page 37;

Homenatge a la Barceloneta © Alexandru Ciobanu, photo 55, page 38;

Beach in Barcelona © Alexandru Ciobanu, photo 56, page 39;

View in Barcelona on Placa De Espanya © Vitalyedush, Dreamstime, photo 57, pages 40 – 41;

Catalonia Square © Jo, Fotolia, photo 58, page 42;

Placa de Catalynia (Square of Catalunia) © Vitalyedush, Dreamstime, photo 59, page 42;

Plaza Real square in the Gothic Quarter in Barcelona © Mari79, Fotolia, photo 60, page 43;

Bullring La Monumental, Barcelona, Spain © Alvaro Trabazo Rivas, Dreamstime, photo 61, page 43;

Panoramic view of La Monumental arena © Alexandru Ciobanu, photo 62, pages 44 - 45;

Barri Gothic Quarter and Bridge of Sighs in Barcelona, Catalonia © Anshar, Canstockphoto, photo 63, pages 46 – 47;

Bridge of Sighs in Barcelona, Catalonia © Anshar, Canstockphoto, photo 64, page 49;

Gothic quarter in Barcelona © Scorpionka, Canstockphoto, photo 65, page 49;

Small street in Barcelona Gothic quarter © Frankix, Fotolia, photo 66, page 49;

Placa del Rei © Alexandru Ciobanu, photo 67, pages 50 - 51;

Facade of Barcelona gothic cathedral, in Spain © Dobled, Canstockphoto, photo 68, page 52;

Barcelona Cathedral Interior, Catalonia, Spain © Bargotiphotography, Canstockphoto, photo 69, page 53;

Statues in the Cathedral of Santa Eulalia in Barcelona © Serystar, Canstockphoto, photo 70, page 53;

Santa Maria del Mar church in Barcelona © Peresanz, Canstockphoto, photo 71, page 54;

Gothic church interior © Perseomedusa, Fotolia, photo 72, page 55;

Els quatre gats restaurant © Alexandru Ciobanu, photo 73, page 56;

Escriba © Alexandru Ciobanu, photo 74, page 57;

Shrimps © Alexandru Ciobanu, photo 75, page 57;

Calamar © Alexandru Ciobanu, photo 76, page 57;

Paella in Barcelona © Alexandru Ciobanu, photo 77, page 57;

Tapas on Crusty Bread © Maksheb, Bigstockphoto, photo 78, page 57;

El Cap de Barcelona © Toni Genes, Dreamstime, photo 79, page 58;

Sculpture Dona i Ocell, Barcelona © 22tomtom, Dreamstime, photo 80, page 58;

Joan Miro's Pla de l'Os mosaic in La Rambla in Barcelona, Spain © Nito, Bigstockphoto, photo 81, page 59;

Fundacio Joan Miro - Barcelona Spain © Catalby, Canstockphoto, photo 82, page 59;

The Picasso Museum in Barcelona, Spain © Maxisports, Bigstockphoto, photo 83, page 60;

Caixa Forum © Alexsalcedo, Canstockphoto, photo 84, page 60;

Maritime Museum, Barcelona © Bambi L. Dingman, Dreamstime, photo 85, page 61;

Gaudi's House Museum © Alexandru Ciobanu, photo 86, page 62;

Forum Building in Barcelona, Spain © Nito, Bigstockphoto, photo 87, page 63;

Barcelona forum © Bernfest, Dreamstime, photo 88, page 63;

National Museum in Barcelona, Placa De Espanya © Ivantagan, Canstockphoto, photo 89, pages 64 – 65;

Buildings in Eixample © Alexandru Ciobanu, photo 90, pages 66 - 67;

Aerial view of Eixample district. Barcelona, Spain © JackF, Canstockphoto, photo 91, pages 68 – 69;

Palau de La Musica Catalana © Alexandre Fagundes De Fagundes, Dreamstime, photo 92, page 70;

Ceiling in Music Palace, Barcelona, Spain © Javarman, Canstockphoto, photo 93, page 70;

Hospital Sant Pau Recinte Modernista. Barcelona, Catalonia, Spain © Ivantagan, Canstockphoto, photo 94, page 71;

Hospital de la Santa Creu i de Sant Pau, Barcelona, Spain © Peresanz, Canstockphoto, photo 95, page 71;

House of the Spikes © Alexandru Ciobanu, photo 96, page 72;

Casa Pamplona © Alexandru Ciobanu, photo 97, page 72;

Street art © Alexandru Ciobanu, photo 98, page 72;

Agbar Tower © 135pixels, Bigstockphoto, photo 99, page 73;

Las arenas shopping center © Alexandru Ciobanu, photo 100, page 74;

Arenas De Barcelona Spain © Alberto SevenOnSeven, Bigstockphoto, photo 101, page 74;

The fish © Alexandru Ciobanu, photo 102, page 74;

Camp Nou stadium © Pljvv, Bigstockphoto, photo 103, page 75;

Aerial cable car at Monjuic hill © Alexandru Ciobanu, photo 104, page 76;

Panoramic view of Barcelona from Montjuic © Alexandru Ciobanu, photo 105, pages 76 - 77;

Panoramic of Cactus Park at Montjuic Barcelona © Pablo Boris Debat, Dreamstime, photo 106, pages 76-77;

View of Castillo de Montjuic © Brian K., photo 107, page 78;

Magic Fountain light show in Barcelona © Bloodua, Canstockphoto, photo 108, page 78;

Parc Olympique, Barcelona © Alexandru Ciobanu, photo 109, page 79;

Houses at Poble Espanyol © Alexandru Ciobanu, photo 110, page 80;

Castle at the Village museum © Alexandru Ciobanu, photo 111, page 81;

Artisan shop at Billage Museum © Alexandru Ciobanu, photo 112, page 82;

Fountain of Parc de la Ciutadella, in Barcelona, Spain © Peresanz, photo 113, page 82;

Triumphal Arch in Barcelona © Alexandru Ciobanu, photo 114, page 83;

People walking at Cervantes Park in Barcelona © Iakov Filimonov, Dreamstime, photo 115, page 84;

A game of pétanque © Alexandru Ciobanu, photo 116, page 84;

Palau Reial de Pedralbes © Nito, Canstockphoto, photo 117, page 85;

Parc de Espanya Industrial © JackF, Canstockphoto, photo 118, page 85;

Cathedral of Pedralbes Monastery at Barcelona © Jack F., Canstockphoto, photo 119, page 86;

Wide view of Antique corridor © Alexandrum01, Dreamstime, photo 120, page 86;

Santa Maria de Montserrat abbey © Yevgen Belich, Bigstockphoto, photo 121, page 87;

Cable Car to Monserrat Monastery © Sergey Kelin, Dreamstime, photo 122, page 87;

Tibidabo church on mountain in Barcelona with Christ statue overviewing the city © Tan4ikk, Bigstockphoto, photo 123, pages 88 – 89;

Interior of Temple Expiatori del Sagrat Cor © GekaSkr, Bigstockphoto, photo 124, page 90;

Roller coaster at Tibidabo. Barcelona © Vladyslav, Canstockphoto, photo 125, page 90;

Amusement Park and Church of the Sacred Heart of Jesus on Mount Tibidabo © Melis, Bigstockphoto, photo 126, page 90;

Blue Hour In Barcelona © Karol Kozlowski, Bigstockphoto, photo 127, page 91.

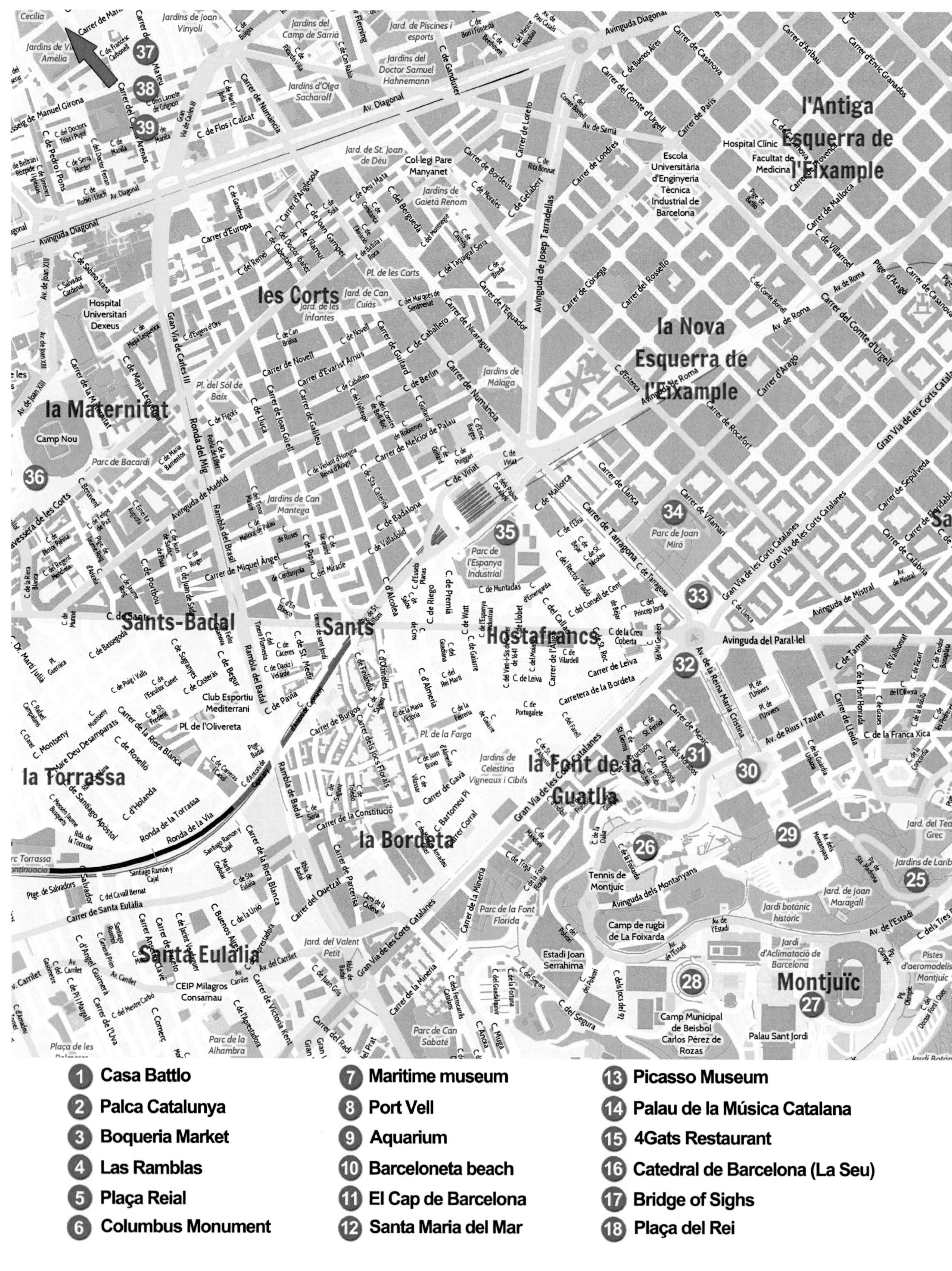
l'Antiga Esquerra de l'Eixample
la Nova Esquerra de l'Eixample
les Corts
la Maternitat
Sants-Badal
Sants
Hostafrancs
la Torrassa
la Font de la Guatlla
la Bordeta
Santa Eulàlia
Montjuïc
Camp Nou
Hospital Universitari Dexeus
Hospital Clínic
Facultat de Medicina
Escola Universitària d'Enginyeria Tècnica Industrial de Barcelona
Col·legi Pare Manyanet
Parc de Joan Miró
Parc de l'Espanya Industrial
Club Esportiu Mediterrani
Tennis de Montjuïc
Camp de rugbi de La Foixarda
Estadi Joan Serrahima
Camp Municipal de Beisbol Carlos Pérez de Rozas
Palau Sant Jordi
CEIP Milagros Consarnau
Avinguda Diagonal
Gran Via de les Corts Catalanes
Avinguda del Paral·lel
Avinguda de Madrid
Avinguda de Josep Tarradellas
Ronda del Mig
Rambla del Brasil
Rambla del Badal
Carrer de Sants
Avinguda de Mistral
1 Casa Battlo
2 Palca Catalunya
3 Boqueria Market
4 Las Ramblas
5 Plaça Reial
6 Columbus Monument
7 Maritime museum
8 Port Vell
9 Aquarium
10 Barceloneta beach
11 El Cap de Barcelona
12 Santa Maria del Mar
13 Picasso Museum
14 Palau de la Música Catalana
15 4Gats Restaurant
16 Catedral de Barcelona (La Seu)
17 Bridge of Sighs
18 Plaça del Rei

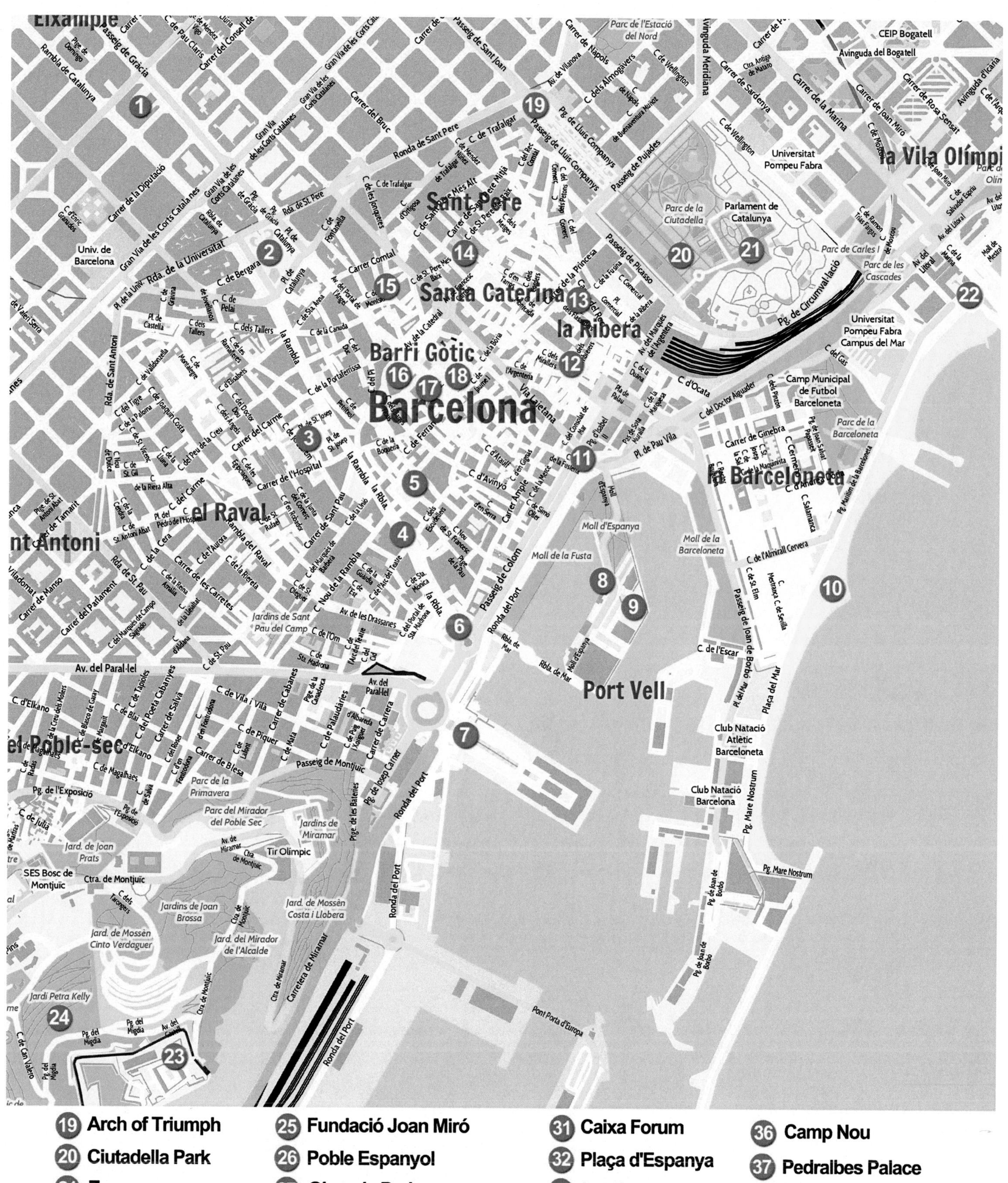

19 Arch of Triumph
20 Ciutadella Park
21 Zoo
22 Peix (Fish)
23 Montjuic Castle
24 Botanic garden
25 Fundació Joan Miró
26 Poble Espanyol
27 Olympic Park
28 Communications Tower
29 National Art Museum
30 Magic fountain of Montjuic
31 Caixa Forum
32 Plaça d'Espanya
33 Las Arenas
34 Joan Miró park
35 Parc de l'Espanya Industrial
36 Camp Nou
37 Pedralbes Palace
38 Parc de Cervantes
39 Monastery of Pedralbes

40 Park Güell

41 Hospital de la Santa Creu i Sant Pau

42 La Sagrada Familia

43 Casa Terrades

44 Casa Milà

45 Arena La Monumental

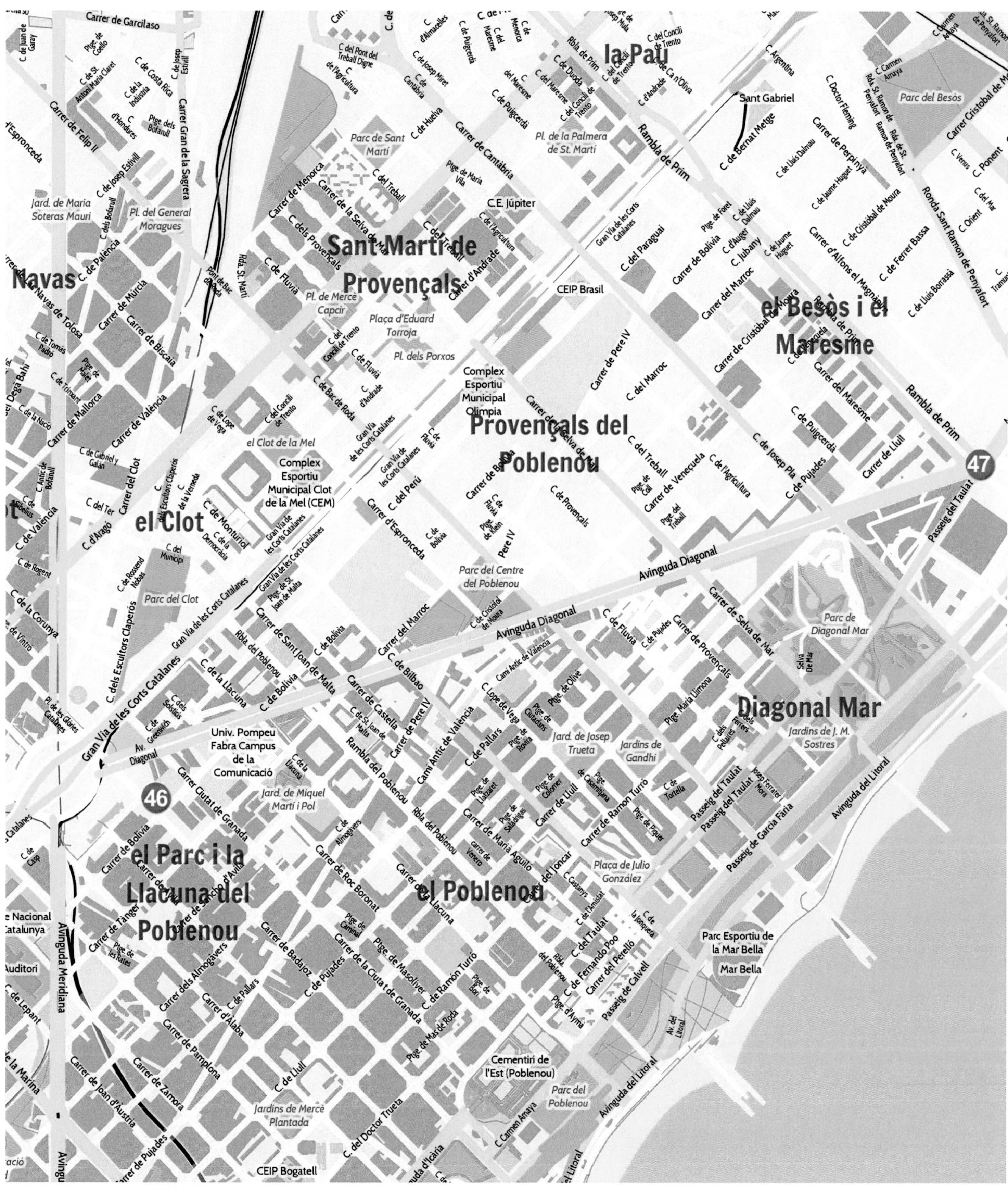

46 **Torre Agbar building**

47 **Forum Building**

48 **Tibidabo**

BARCELONA
A PHOTOGRAPHIC TOUR

First Edition

ISBN-13: 978-1517621162
ISBN-10: 151762116X

From the series Photographic tours

Also available in eBook format

Photographs from this book are available as art prints (framed or unframed) from *www.imagekind.com/artists/AlexandruCiobanu/Barcelona*

Copyright © 2015 by ALEXANDRU CIOBANU
All rights reserved.

alexandru.ciobanu.books@gmail.com

www.alexandru-ciobanu.com
www.alexandruciobanubooks.wordpress.com

Made in the USA
San Bernardino, CA
13 June 2017